FROM SEA to SHINING SEA

# ARIZONA

## CAROLE K. STANDARD

*Consultants*

**MELISSA N. MATUSEVICH, PH.D.**

*Curriculum and Instruction Specialist*
*Blacksburg, Virginia*

**DEBRA LaPLANTE, M.A.**

*Teacher/Librarian*
*Barcelona Primary School*
*Barcelona Middle School*
*Alhambra District*
*Glendale, Arizona*

# CHILDREN'S PRESS®

A DIVISION OF SCHOLASTIC INC.

New York • Toronto • London • Auckland • Sydney • Mexico City
New Delhi • Hong Kong • Danbury, Connecticut

Arizona is in the southwestern part of the United States. It is bordered by New Mexico, Utah, Nevada, California, and Mexico.

Project Editor: Meredith DeSousa
Art Director: Marie O'Neill
Photo Researcher: Marybeth Kavanagh
Design: Robin West, Ox and Company, Inc.
Page 6 map and recipe art: Susan Hunt Yule
All other maps: XNR Productions, Inc.

Library of Congress Cataloging-in-Publication Data

Standard, Carole K.
    Arizona / by Carole K. Standard.
    p. cm. – (From sea to shining sea)
    Includes biographical references and index.
    Summary: Takes readers on a tour of the state and describes its geography, history,
government, people, and places.
    ISBN 0-516-22315-1
    1. Arizona—Juvenile literature. [1. Arizona.] I. Title. II. From sea to shining sea
(Series)

F811.3 .S73 2002
979.1—dc21                              2001032294

# TABLE of CONTENTS

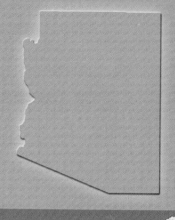

# CHAPTER ONE

# INTRODUCING THE GRAND CANYON STATE

Saguaro cactus (left) and ocotillo (right) are common in the Arizona desert.

**W**hen most people think of Arizona, they think of the Old West and the Grand Canyon. You'll soon discover that there's much more to Arizona. From mountain peaks to desert plains, Arizona is a land full of surprises. It is Native American kachina dolls and rodeos. It is cities with tall buildings and big companies. Behind it all, snow covered mountains tower over green valleys, and colorful rock formations and cacti paint the landscape.

You can learn a lot about Arizona from its state flag. In the center of the flag is a large copper star, because Arizona produces more copper than any other state. Thirteen red and yellow rays extend from the star. Red and yellow are the colors of Spain, a country that claimed the land of Arizona from the mid 1500s until 1821. The thirteen rays may stand for the original thirteen colonies of the United States, or they might represent the thirteen counties that existed in Arizona when the flag was designed in 1911.

Arizona's nickname, the Grand Canyon State, comes from its most famous attraction. The Grand Canyon is one of the most spectacular canyons in the world. Every year, more than four million people visit northwestern Arizona to admire the canyon's beautiful scenery.

What else comes to mind when you think of Arizona?

- A shoot-out between Wyatt Earp and cowboys at the OK Corral
- Astronomers studying the stars and planets at Lowell Observatory and Kitt Peak
- Fans cheering for cowboys at the Prescott Rodeo
- Hikers following trails into the Grand Canyon
- Tourists crossing the London Bridge in Lake Havasu City
- People admiring the spectacular colors of the Painted Desert
- Skiers flying down the slopes at Flagstaff
- Navajo creating colorful sand paintings
- Gila monsters and cacti in the Arizona desert

Although it was once considered a dry, barren desert by some, Arizona is one of the most fascinating and vibrant places in the United States today. Turn the page to discover what makes the Grand Canyon State unique.

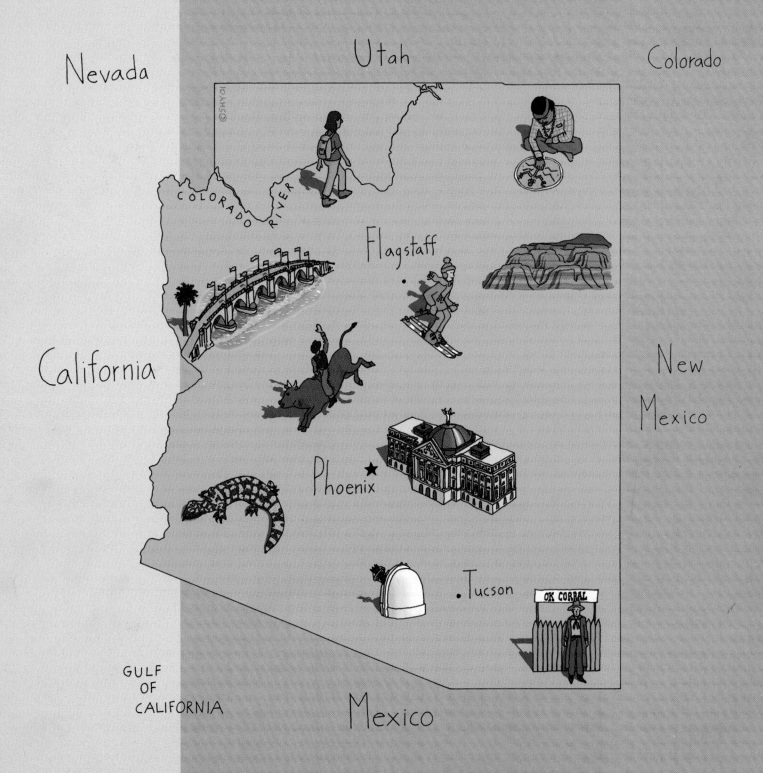

Nevada

Utah

Colorado

California

New
Mexico

Mexico

GULF
OF
CALIFORNIA

COLORADO RIVER

Flagstaff

Phoenix

Tucson

OK CORRAL

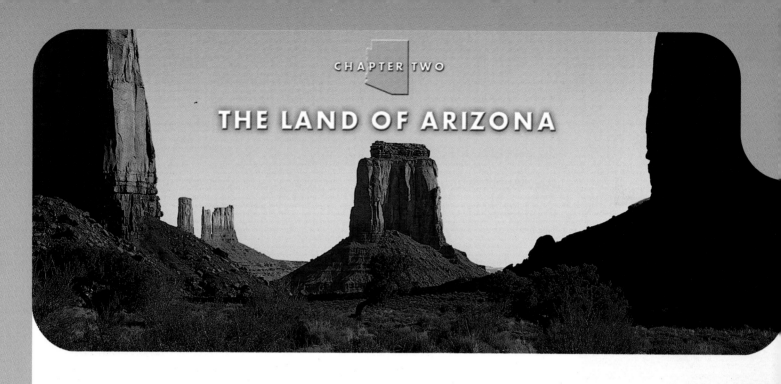

# CHAPTER TWO

# THE LAND OF ARIZONA

**A**rizona is in the southwestern part of the United States. To the west of Arizona lie California and Nevada, and to the south is another country, Mexico. Utah lies to the north of Arizona, and New Mexico lies to the east. The northeastern corner of Arizona touches three states—Utah, Colorado, and New Mexico. The spot where they come together, called Four Corners, is the only place in the United States where four states meet.

Arizona is the sixth largest state. Its total area is 114,007 square miles (295,278 square kilometers). Arizona stretches about four hundred miles (650 kilometers) from north to south and 340 miles (550 km) from east to west at its widest point.

This large area holds an abundance of natural resources. Copper, gold, silver, zinc, mercury, iron, and coal are mined in the state. The one natural resource that Arizona does not have enough of is water. With

The tall, red sandstone buttes of Monument Valley rise as high as 1,000 feet (300 m).

only 364 square miles (943 sq km) of inland water and thirteen inches (33 centimeters) of annual rainfall, it is difficult to provide enough water for everyone. Many laws have been passed to regulate, or control, the use of water in an effort to make sure that enough water will be available for future generations.

## GEOGRAPHIC REGIONS

The land is different across Arizona. There are hot, sandy deserts and cool, snowy mountains. If you were to travel from the northern part of the state to the southern part, you would pass through three different land regions: the Colorado Plateau, the Central Highlands, and the Basin and Range Region.

### The Colorado Plateau

The Colorado Plateau, in the northern part of Arizona, covers about two-fifths of the state. The land in this region is mostly flat and dry, broken up by canyons and mountains. The highest point in the state, Humphreys Peak, is part of the San Francisco Peaks near Flagstaff. It rises 12,633 feet (3,851 meters) from the desert floor.

Millions of years ago, water covered this area. Layers of rock formed under the water. As the water disappeared, rivers were created and cut deep canyons through the land. As a result, the Colorado Plateau is full of colorful canyons and rock formations created long ago. Oak Creek

The beautiful scenery of Oak Creek Canyon draws many visitors.

## FIND OUT MORE

The Grand Canyon is one of seven outstanding natural features of the earth, often referred to as the "Seven Natural Wonders of the World." What are the other six natural wonders? Where are they located?

## FIND OUT MORE

Mesa means "table" in Spanish. Why do you think that these rock formations were called mesas?

(opposite)
The Grand Canyon is a spectacular sight.

Canyon and the Canyon de Chelly were formed by small rivers, called tributaries, that flow into the Colorado River.

One of Arizona's greatest treasures is the Grand Canyon. The Grand Canyon is eighteen miles (29 km) across at its widest point and 277 miles (446 km) long. It is more than five thousand feet (1,525 m)—almost one mile (1.6 km)—deep.

The canyon was created by the Colorado River, which runs through it. Over time the river caused erosion, the gradual wearing away of rock and soil. This process created the rock formations that make up the Grand Canyon, including what are called mesas, or flat-topped rock formations. The mesas are formed from rocks called limestone and sandstone and can sometimes be streaked with colors. Some of the canyon's rock layers are almost two billion years old—the oldest exposed rock in the world.

One area in northeastern Arizona, called the Painted Desert, is full of beautifully colored mesas. Visitors to the desert are amazed by the display of red, purple, blue, yellow, gray, and brown rock. The Painted Desert is part of Petrified Forest National Park, where many ancient fallen logs have turned to stone. Two hundred million years ago, heavy rains pulled many trees out of the ground in the mountains and moved them to the lowlands. The trees were buried under mud, sand, and volcanic ash that caused a chemical change in the wood, turning the trees into stone. These trees are known as petrified wood.

A close-up view of petrified wood reveals an array of bright colors.

Many dinosaur fossils have been found there, as well. In 1984, scientists discovered the bones of a Staurikosaur. Scientists believe that the bones are about 225 million years old—the oldest dinosaur bones ever found. They named this dinosaur *Gertie*.

### The Central Highlands

The Central Highlands (sometimes called the Transitional Zone) is located south of the Colorado Plateau. Most of Arizona's mountains are in the central part of the state. Some of the major mountain ranges are the White Mountains, the Sierra Ancha Mountains, the Santa Maria Mountains, and the Mazatzal Mountains. Many of these mountains have sharp peaks that are made of volcanic ash.

The mountains are rich in minerals. Almost all mining in Arizona is done in this region. Copper, gold, silver, and coal are all mined here.

### The Basin and Range Region

The southern part of Arizona is called the Basin and Range Region. This region is made up of flat, desert plains (the basin) separated by mountain

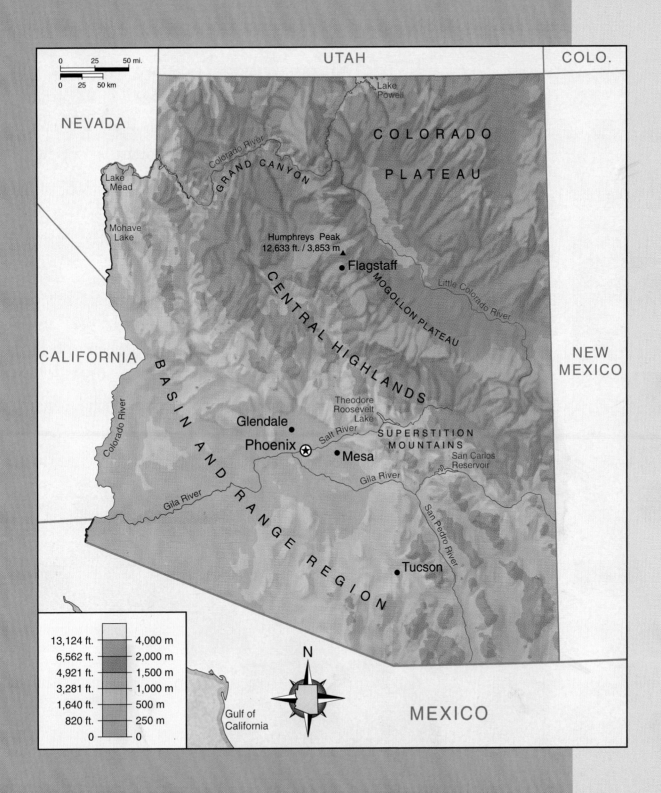

## FIND OUT MORE

We usually think of a desert as a sandy place where nothing grows, but Arizona's desert is full of plants. Find out what types of plants grow in the Arizona desert. How do these plants grow in a place with so little water?

ranges (the range). The land is very good for growing crops, but it requires irrigation, or an artificial water supply, because very little rain falls here. This is the hottest part of the state, where summer temperatures often climb to 100° Fahrenheit (38° Celsius). Most Arizonans live in this region.

The Sonoran Desert extends northward into this region from Mexico. The Sonoran Desert is full of green shrubs and cacti, especially the giant saguaro cactus, whose blooms are the state flower of Arizona. The saguaro cactus is the largest tree in the desert, and it can take up to two hundred years to reach its full height of nearly fifty feet (15 m). Other types of cactus include the cholla, organ pipe, barrel, and prickly pear. Plants such as the yucca, cereus, ironwood, and joshua tree fill the desert with color.

Barrel cactus grow in the Sonoran Desert. Most have yellow-green or red flowers at the top.

Organ pipe cactus can grow as tall as 23 feet (7 m). Its flowers bloom at night.

## RIVERS AND LAKES

The most important river in Arizona is the Colorado River. It enters Arizona from Utah in the north and flows southwest through the Grand Canyon. This 688-mile (1,107-km) river forms a natural border between Arizona and its neighboring states of Nevada and California. Several dams, such as Hoover Dam, have been built on the Colorado River to provide water for Arizonans and to irrigate crops. The Gila River and the Salt River in southern Arizona are also important sources of water for Arizonans.

Rafting down the Colorado River is a fun way to explore Grand Canyon National Park.

In the spring, melting snow from the mountains runs into the rivers, and many rivers become flooded. When there is little rainfall, some of Arizona's rivers may appear to be dry. However, enough water soaks into the soil during floods so that these riverbeds are rarely totally dry.

There are very few natural lakes in Arizona. Many artificial, or manmade, lakes were created by dams built on rivers. Lake Mead, which is shared with Nevada, and Lake Powell, which lies partly in Utah, are two such lakes. Other manmade lakes include Roosevelt Lake and San Carlos Lake.

This aerial view shows Lake Mead and the surrounding mountains.

## CLIMATE

Arizona's climate changes from one region to the next. The mountains have very cold, harsh winters, but desert winters are sunny and mild. Average winter temperatures range from 50°F (10°C) in Phoenix to −25°F (−31°C) in the northern mountains. The lowest recorded temperature in Arizona was −40°F (−40°C) at Hawley Lake on January 7, 1971.

In the summer, people visiting the mountains find cool breezes, while desert hikers discover a hot and dry climate. Summer temperatures in the desert are often scorching, reaching over 100°F (38°C). On June 29, 1994, folks in Lake Havasu City suffered through the hottest day ever recorded in Arizona—a sweltering 128°F (53°C)! Since the air is dry rather than humid (moist), the heat is more bearable than it would be in other parts of the United States.

The mountains receive anywhere from twenty-five to thirty inches (64 to 76 centimeters) of rain each year, but it rarely rains in the southern part of the state. The Sonoran Desert averages only between two and five inches (5 and 13 cm) of rain per year. As much as seventy inches (178 cm) of snow have fallen on the tallest mountains in one year.

# CHAPTER THREE

# ARIZONA THROUGH HISTORY

Rock images, called petroglyphs, were carved by some of the earliest people in Arizona. This one is found along the Little Colorado River.

**P**eople have lived in present-day Arizona for more than twelve thousand years. The first people, called Paleo-Indians, arrived from the north. They hunted mammoths, bison, and bear, using spears made from rocks. These people were nomads, moving around the grassy plains to follow the animals they hunted. Eventually, the animals became more and more scarce, and the people began eating wild fruits and berries. No one knows exactly what happened to the Paleo-Indians, but they gradually disappeared.

The next known people of this region were called the Anasazi. The Anasazi lived in the northwest part of the state about two thousand years ago. They grew their

## FIND OUT MORE

A mammoth was a large, elephant-like animal that lived in North America thousands of years ago. Since then, these creatures have mysteriously disappeared. Scientists have several theories, or ideas, as to what caused their disappearance, including disease and changes in climate. How might humans have contributed to their extinction?

own food, including corn, beans, and squash. The early Anasazi made baskets to carry water and food. Later, they made clay pots and used the pots for cooking.

In the beginning, the Anasazi built permanent homes out of clay and adobe, a type of brick that is made from soil and straw and then dried in the sun. The Anasazi built their homes together in groups that looked like small cities, called *pueblos.* They also built round underground rooms called *kivas,* which were probably used for religious ceremonies or social gatherings. Colorful mural paintings filled the walls of the kivas, showing religious figures or scenes of daily life.

The remains of elaborate Anasazi cliff dwellings can be explored at Mesa Verde National Park.

Over time, the Anasazi moved out of their homes and into what became known as cliff dwellings. These dwellings ranged from small spaces (one-room houses) to large villages (more than two hundred rooms) that were carved into stone cliffs. Remains of the cliff dwellings can still be seen in Mesa Verde.

In A.D. 300, another group known as the Hohokam traveled from Mexico and settled in central Arizona. These Native Americans were farmers who learned to grow corn (known as maize) in Mexico.

Later the Hohokam also grew squash, beans, and cotton. They developed a way to water their crops using ditches.

Both the Anasazi and the Hohokam people thrived until around A.D. 1300, when a long drought occurred. It became difficult to grow food without water, and as a result many of these people died. The remainder of the groups moved away in search of a new source of water.

By the time the first Europeans arrived, two Native American groups, the Pima and the Papago, lived in the south central part of the region. The tribes were descendants of the Hohokam and Mogollan people, who lived in the area near Tucson. The Hopi tribe lived in the northeast.

## EUROPEAN EXPLORATION

In 1539, Marcos de Niza, a Spanish monk from Mexico City, traveled into Arizona and New Mexico. He came in search of wealthy cities that were thought to be in the area. He later claimed to have found the cities in a province called Cíbola, in present-day New Mexico. Legend said that the streets of Cíbola were paved with gold and jewels. De Niza, however, never entered the city and instead returned to Mexico.

In 1540, de Niza served as a guide for Spanish explorer Francisco Vásquez de Coronado and his men. Coronado also came to Arizona in search of gold and riches. The group found a city called Cíbola, but the streets were not paved in gold as they had hoped. Instead, Cíbola was a Native American village with homes made of mud. Although

Coronado led hundreds of Spaniards, Native Americans, and animals on an expedition through the North American southwest.

they never discovered any riches, they explored many important physical landmarks in the area. One of Coronado's men, García López de Cárdenas, was the first European to discover the Grand Canyon. Coronado's discoveries later served as the basis for Spanish claim to Arizona.

In 1629, Roman Catholic priests known as missionaries arrived in northern Arizona. They began building missions that included a fort and a church, as well as houses, farm buildings, and a school. The purpose of these missions was to convert the Hopi to the Catholic religion. The Hopi, however, worshiped spirits called *kachinas*. The Hopi did not want to give up their religion and they eventually became angry with the missionaries for their forceful attempts to control the Hopi. In 1680, the Hopi attacked the missions and killed many Europeans.

## WHO'S WHO IN ARIZONA?

**Francisco Vásquez de Coronado (1510–1554)** was a Spanish explorer. In search of gold and riches, he led what would later become one of the most significant European explorations of western North America. Coronado's expedition explored many parts of the southwest, including Arizona and New Mexico.

Not all of the missionaries were disliked by Native Americans. In 1687, Eusebio Francisco Kino, known as "the Padre on Horseback," opened a successful mission in southern Arizona. He taught Native Americans new ways to farm and how to raise cattle.

During the early 1700s, many Spanish people traveled from Mexico to settle in Arizona. As more settlers moved in, they took land that belonged to Native Americans. Settlers and Native Americans fought over land claims. In 1752, the Spanish built the first *presidio,* or fort, at Tubac to protect the settlers. It was the first permanent European settlement in Arizona. Later, the fort was moved north to what is now Tucson.

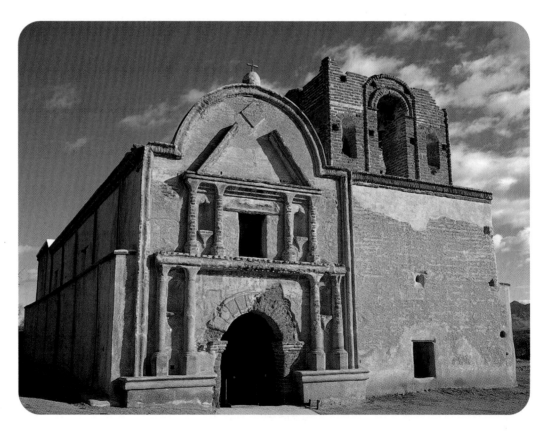

San José de Tumacácori mission, built in 1691, is one of the oldest Spanish missions in Arizona.

At this time, Arizona was part of Mexico, which belonged to Spain. Mexico, however, wanted to be free from Spanish rule. They fought for their freedom and won independence in 1821. The treaty (agreement) that ended the war gave the land that is now Arizona to Mexico.

Mexico now controlled a large part of the southwest. As the number of American settlers, fur trappers, and traders in this area increased, the United States government wanted the territory as its own. Mexico did not want to give up its claims and as a result, war broke out between the United States and Mexico in 1846.

When the Mexican War (1846–1848) ended, Mexico ceded, or gave up, its right to these lands. The United States now controlled the northern part of Arizona, in addition to the present-day areas of California, Nevada, Utah, Texas, and parts of Colorado, New Mexico, and Wyoming. Together, all this land was declared part of the Territory of New Mexico in 1850.

In 1853, the United States government purchased the southern parts of New Mexico and Arizona from Mexico for $10 million. This strip of land was known as the Gadsden Purchase, named after James Gadsden, who negotiated the deal. This land was important to the United States because it was the most practical route for a railroad line to the Pacific Ocean. Arizona in its entirety was now completely claimed by the United States.

James Gadsden wanted to purchase southern Arizona from Mexico in order to build a railroad through the territory.

In 1851, the United States Army Corps of Engineers began exploring Arizona to find the best route for a wagon trail to California. Army posts were built along the route to protect travelers from Native Americans. The wagon trail later became a railroad route. Arizona served as a key link between California and the midwestern states.

In the 1850s, miners from other states made their way to Arizona. It wasn't long before gold was discovered on the Gila River, silver was found in Globe, and copper was uncovered in Bisbee. The miners' success led to a period of growth. The population jumped from 30,388 in 1830 to 435,450 in 1860. Mining communities were set up, and towns grew around them. Miners needed food and supplies, so farmers began to grow crops and raise cattle. Phoenix became a trading post for miners and their families.

Phoenix was a bustling city in the late 1800s. This photo shows a street in the main part of town.

In 1863, President Abraham Lincoln made Arizona a separate territory. John Goodwin was named territorial governor and Prescott became the first capital. In 1867, the capital was moved to Tucson, and finally, in 1889, to Phoenix, which is still the capital today.

Arizona's population grew so quickly that many of the mining towns became dangerous. Laws were frequently broken and ignored. Arguments were settled with fights and shootouts. Famous lawmen such as Wyatt Earp fought to enforce the laws.

Not all criminals were men. One of Arizona's most notorious female criminals was Pearl Hart. In 1898, Hart and a miner named Joe Boot robbed a stagecoach. The pair took almost $500 from the coach and were captured several days later. Pearl was put in jail, but she escaped and was soon recaptured. During her trial, Pearl admitted her guilt, yet the jury found her innocent. The judge was furious and ordered a new trial, stating that Pearl had ". . . flirted with the jury, bending them to her will." He selected a new

jury and retried her on different charges. Pearl was found guilty and sentenced to five years in the Yuma Territorial Prison.

## ARIZONA'S INDIAN WARS

The continuing population growth in Arizona forced many Native Americans from their land. In addition, most settlers felt that Native Americans should give up their traditions and customs and become more like white Americans. In an effort to keep what was theirs, Native Americans, particularly the Apache and the Navajo, fought fiercely against white settlers. Bloody battles went on for many years.

The conflict continued even during the Civil War (1861–1865). As the northern states fought the southern states over the issue of slavery, the Navajo raided white settlements and other Native American settlements. In 1863, a New Mexico military officer named Kit Carson waged his own war on the Arizona Navajo. His troops, along with some Hopi, Pueblo, Utes, and Zuni, marched through Navajo territory and destroyed crops, livestock, and orchards. Without food supplies, the Navajo were left to starve. They surrendered in 1864, and more than eight thousand Navajo were forced to walk three hundred miles (483 km) from Arizona to Fort Sumner, New Mexico, where they were held prisoner at Bosque Redondo Reservation. Many Navajo died of disease and starvation during what became known as "the long walk." In 1868 they were allowed to return to a reservation in the Four Corners region of Arizona.

In 1863, Kit Carson destroyed Navajo territory in Arizona.

Two fierce Chiricahua Apache warriors, Cochise and Geronimo, continued to fight long after other tribes had surrendered. When Geronimo finally surrendered to United States Army troops in 1877, he was jailed in a Florida prison and was later held at Fort Sill in Oklahoma. Geromino wrote to President Grant, requesting that he be allowed to live peacefully in the hills of Arizona. "It is my land, my home, my father's land, to which I now ask to be allowed to return," he wrote. "I want to spend my last days there, and be buried among those mountains. If this could be I might die in peace, feeling that my people, placed in their native homes, would increase in numbers, rather than diminish as at present, and that our name would not become extinct." He was not allowed to return, however, and Geronimo died at Fort Sill in 1909.

Native Americans were moved onto reservations, or public lands set aside by the government specifically for their use. They were watched and restricted in their movements. Because they were not permitted to hunt freely, they were unable to provide for themselves and were forced to rely on government assistance.

In 1887, the Dawes General Allotment Act allowed reservation land to be divided up among tribesmen so that Native Americans could become farmers. Men with families received 160 acres (65 hectares) of land. The Act also allowed for the sale of any extra reservation land to non-Native Americans. While the Dawes Act was meant to help Native Americans, it did just the opposite. Instead, they lost millions of acres of land across the United States because of this act. In addition, much of the land they were given was not suitable for farming, and in any case, many Native Americans could not afford tools and supplies that were necessary for farming.

George W. P. Hunt served seven terms as Arizona's governor.

## ARIZONA BECOMES A STATE

In 1912, Arizona had a population of more than 215,000. Arizonans were ready for statehood, but they had to convince Congress to allow it. A few years earlier, Congress suggested that Arizona join with New Mexico to become one state, but Arizonans rejected the idea. Finally, on February 14, 1912, Arizona was admitted as the forty-eighth state. Arizona's entry into the Union completed what is referred to as the 'continental' United States—the forty-eight states that share borders with each other. The first elected governor of Arizona was George Wiley Paul Hunt.

One of the biggest problems for the new state was a shortage of water. Roosevelt Dam, which was completed in 1911, was the first of several dams that would be built to address this problem. The dam was

part of a larger plan called the Salt River Project, which would control the flow of the Salt River and allow it to be used for irrigation. The dam was a huge success and turned dry Arizona land into land that was suitable for farming.

Governor Hunt supported the building of dams, and within the next thirty years the Coolidge Dam, the Bartlett Dam, and the Hoover Dam were built. These dams not only helped to provide irrigation for farm-

It took eight years to build the Roosevelt Dam. The dam's unique arch design earned it a place on the National Register of Historic Places.

29

## FIND OUT MORE

Today there are fifty states in the nation. Which two states joined the Union after Arizona? When did they become states? In what ways are a state and a territory different?

ing, but also water and electricity for use by all Arizonans. Hunt also directed the building of highways across the state, which attracted still more people to Arizona.

## WORLD WAR I AND THE GREAT DEPRESSION

In 1914, World War I (1914–1918) broke out among several European nations. The United States became involved in the war partly because of an incident related to Arizona. In 1917, British officials found a German telegram asking for Mexico's help in the war. In return, Germany promised to give Texas, Arizona, and New Mexico back to Mexico when, and if, Germany was successful. The note angered the United States government. The United States entered the war and fought against the Germans, helping the Allies to win the war.

In 1929, hard times hit the United States. In October of that year, many people lost huge amounts of money in their business investments. As a result, they could no longer afford to buy goods, and many businesses failed because they couldn't sell enough products. In Arizona, businesses and banks were forced to close, leaving thousands of people without jobs. People panicked as their savings were lost, and the country plunged into a period of hard times called the Great Depression.

The Depression forced people all over the country to move around in search of work, and some of them settled in Arizona. Its population grew from about 330,000 in 1920 to almost 500,000 in 1940. However, Arizona suffered hard times along with the rest of the states, and there were simply not enough jobs available for everyone.

In an effort to get the nation back on its feet, President Franklin Roosevelt created the Civilian Conservation Corps (CCC). The CCC put thousands of people back to work building new roads, bridges, parks, and buildings throughout the United States. In Arizona, some of the CCC's projects included Colossal Cave Mountain Park in Tucson and the Lowell Ranger Station in the Santa Catalina Mountains.

## WORLD WAR II

The United States began recovering from the Great Depression in 1939, when World War II (1939–1945) began. On December 7, 1941, the Japanese bombed Pearl Harbor, a U.S. Naval base in Hawaii. More than 1,100 crew members died when the USS *Arizona* was sunk. Because of this attack, the United States entered the war that year.

The war created new demand for products and food. Cotton grown in Arizona was used to make uniforms. Farmers raised cattle to feed the troops. Defense industries developed in Arizona. The Army trained many of its pilots at Arizona military bases. When many men left the state to fight with the armed forces, women filled their jobs

The Navajo code talkers transmitted messages by telephone and radio in their native language.

and kept the economy running smoothly.

Arizona's Navajo people made a major contribution to the war effort. When the United States entered the war, military officers needed a way to send secret messages in code. Philip Johnston, the son of a missionary on a Navajo reservation, suggested the use of the Navajo language. Very few non-Navajos could speak the difficult language and it was virtually impossible to translate. The Navajo code talkers, as they were called, attended boot camp to set up a dictionary for military terms. They were then sent to work with the United States Marines in the Pacific.

The Navajo code talkers' success was legendary. Six Navajos worked nonstop for two days during an important battle at Iwo Jima, sending more than eight hundred messages without a mistake. Army Major Howard Connor said, "Were it not for the Navajos, the Marines would have

This monument in honor of the Navajo code talkers is located in Phoenix.

never taken Iwo Jima." While the Japanese had previously broken codes used by the Army and the Air Force, they were never able to decipher the Navajo code.

## DISCRIMINATION IN ARIZONA

Despite their value to the war effort, Native Americans were still not treated as equals in Arizona. They were not forced to remain on their reservations, but they were also not welcomed as a part of society. Many Native Americans did not continue their education and, as a result, had lower paying jobs.

Over time, Native Americans fought for their rights. Although the Snyder Act of 1924 granted citizenship to all Native Americans born in the United States, Arizona's Native Americans were still not permitted to vote because it was left up to individual states to decide who had the right to vote. In 1948, after a lengthy court battle, the state supreme court finally overturned a law that kept Native Americans from voting.

Mexican-Americans and African-Americans were also discriminated against, or set apart from others, in Arizona. They often lived in poor neighborhoods with bad housing and usually attended separate schools from whites. In 1954, the United States Supreme Court ruled that the segregation, or separation, of blacks and whites in schools was unconstitutional. Mexican-Americans also benefited from this ruling. Both groups were then allowed to attend school with whites.

While their treatment improved somewhat, there was still prejudice in Arizona. Even in the 1960s, businesses discriminated against Native Americans. Reservation life segregated them from the rest of Arizona's population. Eventually, they began to open stores and start businesses on their reservations. The first Native American college in the country, Diné College, opened in 1969 on the Navajo Reservation in Tsaile. In the 1980s, President Ronald Reagan passed laws to allow gambling on reservations. Some tribes opened casinos that have led to economic growth, resulting in

This Navajo boy watches over a case of jewelry at a shop on his reservation.

more money for health, education, and other things.

Mexican-Americans, too, fought to overcome prejudice. In the 1960s, they began to embrace their culture and traditions. They proudly called themselves *chicano*, a slang term that comes from the Spanish word *Mexicanos*.

## MODERN TIMES

Arizona's population has grown quickly since the 1970s. One of the reasons for this rapid growth was the widespread use of home air conditioning. As air conditioners became available and affordable, people felt more comfortable living in the extreme desert heat of southern Arizona.

A continual problem for Arizona is the ability to provide enough water for its needs. Water conservation is more than fixing a leaky faucet—it is a way of life for Arizonans. The state is continually finding new ways to handle the problem. In 1974, the Central Arizona Project was designed to bring water from the Colorado River to Phoenix and Tucson. More than three hundred miles (483 km) of pipeline was laid

## WHAT'S IN A NAME?

Many names of places in Arizona have interesting origins.

| Name | Comes From or Means |
|---|---|
| Arizona | From the Native American word *arizonac*, meaning "little spring" or "young spring" |
| Flagstaff | Named for the pine tree that was used to hold a flag for the Independence Day celebration in 1876 |
| Phoenix | Named for the mythical bird that rose from its own ashes |
| Yuma | From the Yuman word *uma*, meaning "fire" |
| Tombstone | Named by Edward Schieffelin, who was told that "all you'll find is your own tombstone" when he mined in the area |
| Tucson | Originally *Stjukshon*, a Native American word meaning "spring at the foot of black mountain" |
| Santa Catalina Mountains | Named by Father Kino in the late 1600s—originally known as the Santa Catarina Mountains |
| Sabino Canyon | Believed to come from the Spanish word *sabino*, referring to a reddish color in the rocks |

## FIND OUT MORE

Many people do not realize how much water they use. Did you know that:
- flushing a toilet uses 1.6–7 gallons of water?
- a five-minute shower uses 12.5–50 gallons of water?
- the average person uses 123 gallons of water each day? According to this figure, how many gallons of water would four people use in a month?

Some Columbia University students spend a semester at Biosphere to study geology and the environment.

across the state, costing more than $4 billion. Arizona's government has also passed strict water conservation laws to help manage water use in the state. The Groundwater Management Act, passed in 1980, helped educate Arizona citizens about the importance of conserving water.

Arizonans also have an interest in their environment. Not far from Tucson is the largest living laboratory in the world—Biosphere 2. Biosphere 2 is located in Oracle, in the Sonoran Desert. Inside the Biosphere are several ecosystems including that of a rain forest, a salt water ocean, and a desert. In 1991, a group of scientists was sealed inside Biosphere 2 for two years to determine whether humans could live within a closed ecosystem. The experiment was not successful, but the Biosphere has since been used as a research facility to help scientists and students learn about the earth and its future.

## PRECIOUS LAND

Just as water is precious to most Arizonans, land is precious to Native American groups in Arizona. A recent conflict focused on Sugarloaf Mountain in the San Francisco Peaks. Much of the stone that is used to make stonewashed denim jeans is taken from a mine on Sugarloaf Mountain. Thirteen Native American tribes fought to limit the mining because of its effect on the Peaks, which are sacred to many tribes. In August 2000, federal officials agreed to close the mine, a victory for both the Navajo and Hopi tribes. The Peaks are one of the four borders of the universe for the Navajo, while the Hopi believe that kachina spirits live in the mountains as clouds and bring rain.

Another land conflict is taking place in the Santa Rita Mountains, south of Tucson. The Smithsonian Institution plans to construct a multi-million dollar telescope project on land that is considered sacred by Native Americans. The location was chosen for the telescopes because the mountains help to shield the city lights. The site, called a Sweat Lodge, has been used for traditional Native American ceremonies such as weddings and prayer meetings.

In 2000, President Clinton signed a bill creating the Agua Fria National Monument, forty miles (64 km) north of

Agua Fria National Monument includes 71,000 acres (28,733 ha) of semi-desert land.

37

Phoenix. The ancient Native American ruins within Agua Fria contain rock carvings called petroglyphs that preserve the history and heritage of the Hopi people who once lived there. Agua Fria will help to educate future generations about Arizona's past.

Arizona is no longer a rough and rugged frontier. It is a thriving state where traditions from the past blend with the advances of the present. The creation of national parks guarantee that future generations will also be able to enjoy Arizona's natural beauty.

# CHAPTER FOUR

# GOVERNING ARIZONA

**A**rizona's government is based on its constitution, a document that outlines the principles by which a state is governed. Arizona's constitution was adopted in 1911. Since then, it has been amended, or changed, more than ninety times as the needs of the people change.

Arizona's government is organized in a way similar to the United States government. It is made up of three branches, or parts: the executive branch, legislative branch, and judicial branch. All of these branches operate separately but work together to keep the state running smoothly.

Arizona's state capitol was turned into a museum in 1981. It also holds the state archives.

## EXECUTIVE BRANCH

The executive branch is responsible for enforcing the state's laws. The governor is the head of the executive branch. He or she is elected by the people of Arizona to serve a four-year term. The governor cannot serve for more than eight years.

The governor is responsible for making sure that the laws of Arizona are followed. All bills (proposed laws) are presented to the governor, who has the right to veto a bill and refuse to sign it into law. Arizona's governor is also the commander-in-chief of the state militia, and can call them to action in an emergency.

Other positions in the executive branch include the secretary of state, the treasurer, the attorney general, and a superintendent of public instruction. All of these officials are elected for four years.

## LEGISLATIVE BRANCH

The legislative branch is responsible for making the state's laws. This branch is made up of two parts: the senate and the house of representatives. The senate has thirty members and the house of representatives has sixty members. These lawmakers, or legislators, are elected by the people of Arizona to serve two-year terms.

Arizona's legislators meet once a year starting on the second Monday of January to discuss proposed new laws, which are called bills. They consider bills related to education, taxes, and the environment, among other things. An idea for a new law may come from legislators, businesses, and citizens of Arizona. Every bill must be voted on by both the senate and the house of representatives. It is then sent to the governor for his or her approval.

## ARIZONA GOVERNORS

| Name | Term | Name | Term |
|------|------|------|------|
| George W. P. Hunt | 1912–1917 | John Howard Pyle | 1951–1955 |
| Thomas E. Campbell | 1917 | Ernest W. McFarland | 1955–1959 |
| George W. P. Hunt | 1918 | Paul Fannin | 1959–1965 |
| Thomas E. Campbell | 1919–1923 | Samuel P. Goddard, Jr. | 1965–1967 |
| George W. P. Hunt | 1923–1929 | John R. "Jack" Williams | 1967–1975 |
| John C. Phillips | 1929–1931 | Raul H. Castro | 1975–1977 |
| George W. P. Hunt | 1931–1933 | Harvey Wesley Bolin | 1977–1978 |
| Benjamin B. Moeur | 1933–1937 | Bruce Babbitt | 1978–1987 |
| Rawghlie C. Stanford | 1937–1939 | Evan Mecham | 1987–1988 |
| Robert T. Jones | 1939–1941 | Rose Mofford | 1988–1991 |
| Sidney P. Osborn | 1941–1948 | Fife Symington | 1991–1997 |
| Daniel E. Garvey | 1948–1951 | Jane Hull | 1997– |

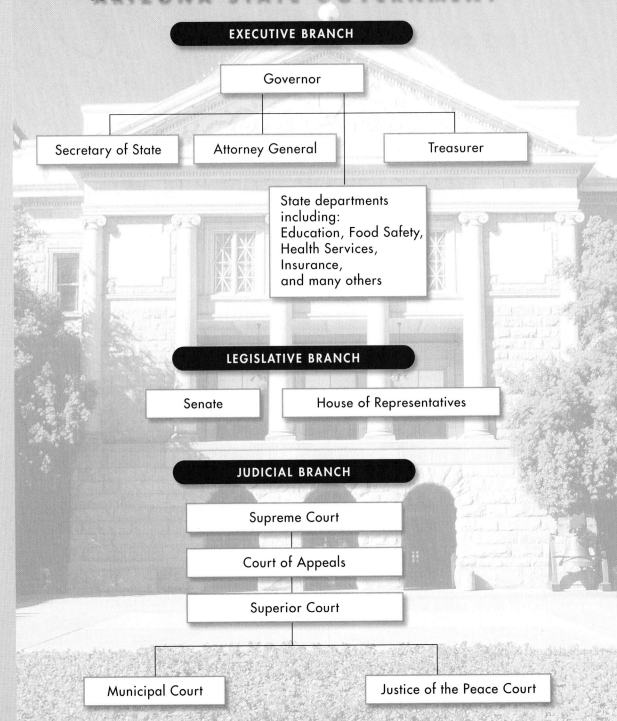

# ARIZONA STATE GOVERNMENT

## EXECUTIVE BRANCH

Governor

Secretary of State

Attorney General

Treasurer

State departments including:
Education, Food Safety,
Health Services,
Insurance,
and many others

## LEGISLATIVE BRANCH

Senate

House of Representatives

## JUDICIAL BRANCH

Supreme Court

Court of Appeals

Superior Court

Municipal Court

Justice of the Peace Court

## JUDICIAL BRANCH

The judicial branch interprets the state's laws through the court system. Many cases begin in either municipal court or a justice of the peace court. These courts hear cases that involve less serious offenses, such as traffic violations. If one of the participants is not satisfied with the court's decision, they can appeal, or take their case to a higher court. Other cases begin in superior courts, which hear both civil cases (those involving a violation of rights) and criminal cases (those in which a law has been broken).

Beyond the superior court is the state court of appeals and the supreme court, the highest court in Arizona. Five justices (judges) are appointed by the governor to serve a six-year term on the supreme court. After that, the people vote on whether or not a justice will serve another term. The justices elect one member to serve as chief justice.

This photo shows the city skyline of Phoenix.

## TAKE A TOUR OF PHOENIX, THE STATE CAPITAL

Located in the south central part of the state on the Salt River, Phoenix is Arizona's largest city. In fact, with more than 1,300,000 residents, it is the seventh-largest city in the United States.

Phoenix is a major agricultural center. Cotton, citrus fruit, dates, olives, and other crops are grown in the area. The electronics, communications, and aerospace industries are important to the Phoenix economy.

One of the city's highlights is the capitol building. The capitol building was completed in 1900, and additions were made in 1919 and 1938. Fifteen tons of copper cover the capitol roof and dome, and a statue called "Winged Victory" stands on top of the dome. The statue is a windvane and changes direction according to the wind. Over the years, Arizona's government outgrew the capitol building and in 1974 the government offices were moved to other locations. Today, the building serves as the Arizona State Capitol Museum.

Inside the capitol, the Arizona state seal is set in tiles on the floor of the rotunda.

45

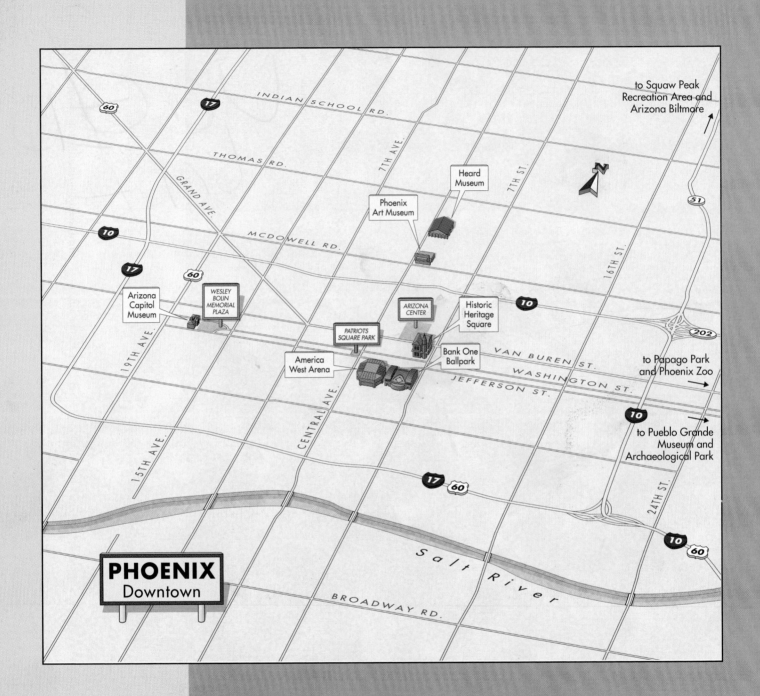

to Squaw Peak
Recreation Area and
Arizona Biltmore

INDIAN SCHOOL RD.

THOMAS RD.

Heard
Museum

Phoenix
Art Museum

McDOWELL RD.

GRAND AVE.

7TH AVE.

7TH ST.

16TH ST.

51

202

to Papago Park
and Phoenix Zoo

Arizona
Capitol
Museum

WESLEY
BOLIN
MEMORIAL
PLAZA

ARIZONA
CENTER

Historic
Heritage
Square

PATRIOTS
SQUARE PARK

Bank One
Ballpark

America
West Arena

VAN BUREN ST.

WASHINGTON ST.

JEFFERSON ST.

to Pueblo Grande
Museum and
Archaeological Park

19TH AVE.

15TH AVE.

CENTRAL AVE.

24TH ST.

10

60

10

60

Salt River

BROADWAY RD.

**PHOENIX**
Downtown

Also in Phoenix is the Heard Museum, the nation's leading museum of Native American art and culture. Its display on "Native Peoples of the Southwest" has won many awards. Jewelry, pottery, crafts, and kachina dolls are among the many Native American items on exhibit. More Native American crafts are displayed at the Pueblo Grande Museum and Archaeological Park. Exhibits include a prehistoric Hohokam ruin, as well as arts and crafts such as pottery and baskets.

Finely woven baskets (above) and kachina dolls (left) are just a few of the Native American crafts on display at the Heard Museum.

If you like the old west, spend some time at the Pioneer Arizona Living History Museum. This 'museum' is actually a reproduction of an 1800s town, where you can see an old sheriff's office and jail, a blacksmith shop, and a miner's cabin. Costumed cowboys and sheriffs roam the town streets.

Other museums include the Phoenix Art Museum, which exhibits Latin American and Western American art, and the Arizona Doll and Toy Museum, where

47

you'll find a collection of dolls from other countries. The Hall of Flame Museum of Firefighting has one of the largest displays of fire fighting equipment in the world. Hand-pulled, horse-drawn, and motorized fire engines are on display.

Papago Park is home to both the Desert Botanical Garden and the Phoenix Zoo. The Desert Botanical Garden has one of the world's largest collections of desert plants, including cactus and desert wild-

A walk through the Desert Botanical Garden reveals a vast amount of life in the Arizona desert.

flowers. There's plenty to see and do at the Phoenix Zoo, where more than 1,300 animals are housed. You can take a behind-the-scenes tour of the zoo to see the animals up close and talk to the zookeepers. You can even spend the night there and take a night hike, where you might run into some bats and owls.

Phoenix is also home to many students. Arizona State University has a branch campus in northwest Phoenix. More than five thousand students attend ASU West.

# CHAPTER FIVE

# THE PEOPLE AND PLACES OF ARIZONA

Arizonans browse at an arts festival in Sedona.

**M**ore than five million people live in Arizona. It is one of the fastest-growing states in the nation. Between 1990 and 2000, Arizona's population grew by almost half. Most of the state's residents—more than eight of every ten people—live in cities. Phoenix is the largest city, and Mesa, Glendale, Tempe, and Scottsdale are all part of the Phoenix metropolitan area. More than half the population of Arizona lives in these cities.

The people of Arizona are very diverse. About seventy-five of every hundred Arizonans are of European descent. Hispanics make up twenty-five of every one hundred people, three of every hundred are African-American, and two of every hundred are Asian American. More than eleven of every hundred Arizonans belong to other ethnic groups. About 300,000 Native Americans live in Arizona.

## HISPANICS

Arizona has a large Hispanic population, which flavors the art, culture, and cuisine of the state. Mexican holidays, such as El Dieciseis de Septiembre (Mexico's Independence Day), are celebrated across Arizona. Cinco de Mayo celebrates the Mexican defeat of the French at the Battle of Puebla on May 5, 1862. Cinco de Mayo celebrations in Arizona are as large as those held in Mexican cities.

It is projected that, by the year 2025, one in every three Arizonans will be Hispanic. Today's Hispanic population has challenges to overcome. In 1990, Hispanic children were three times more likely to be poor than non-Hispanic white children. The school dropout rate for Hispanic teenagers was almost more than twice that of the white non-Hispanic population. Many Hispanics have lower incomes and no health care.

Arizona's government has created legislation to help strengthen Hispanic families. Laws have been passed that will help provide a strong educational background for young children and their parents. Efforts to help Hispanics continue their education and receive training will help raise family incomes. Making Hispanic families aware of the programs available to them will help improve their quality of life.

Traditional Mexican dance is just one of the festivities at La Fiesta de Tumacacori, a two-day festival that celebrates various cultures in Arizona.

Arizona has the second largest population of Native Americans in the United States, after Oklahoma. The Navajo nation is the largest; other nations include the Hopi, Apache, Pima, Yuma, Havasupai, Mohave, Maricopa, Tohono O'Odham, and the Walapai.

There are twenty Native American reservations in the state. Most Native Americans live on these reservations. The Navajo Reservation is the largest in the United States. It covers the northeastern corner of Arizona and stretches into New Mexico and Utah. The reservation is larger than Rhode Island, Connecticut, Vermont, and New Hampshire combined.

Navajo life is focused around their homes, called hogans. Many years ago, hogans were made of three poles laced together at the top and covered with sticks and mud. Today, hogans are made of logs and have eight sides. Most hogans have electricity.

The Navajo are famous for sand painting. Navajo medicine men create sand paintings on the floor of a ceremonial hogan to help cure a sick person. The drawings, which show Navajo gods, are done at night during a ritual called a

A traditional hogan is made of logs bonded together with cement.

"sing." Just before dawn, the sacred pictures are destroyed, and the sand is collected and buried.

The Hopi Reservation is located within the Navajo Reservation. The Hopi live in eleven villages on high mesas. One village, Oraibi, is thought to be the oldest village in the United States in which people have lived continuously.

The Hopi are well known for their kachina dolls. Kachinas are often carved from cottonwood and are considered sacred. They represent ancient spirits.

These Navajo Indians are creating a traditional sand painting on the floor of a hogan.

53

### Service Industry

Almost three of every ten Arizona workers are employed in service jobs, or jobs that provide assistance to the public. Jobs in the service industry include accounting, real estate, finance, and health care, among other things. Phoenix is a major financial center for the state. Almost fifteen of every hundred people work for the government. These people work at military bases such as Fort Huachuca Military Reservation or Williams Air Force Base, and on Native American reservations.

Since World War II, tourism has become an important part of Arizona's service industry. Tourism is the business of providing food, shelter, and entertainment for visitors. People from all over the world travel to Arizona to see the state's many natural wonders, such as the Grand Canyon and the Petrified Forest. More than twenty million people visit Arizona each year.

### Farming

Arizona's rich soil has made farming an important industry. There are almost eight thousand farms in the state. The warm winters make it possible for farmers to grow fruits and vegetables all year long. Crops grown in Arizona include lettuce, broccoli, citrus fruits, melons, grapes, cauliflower, hay, corn, and cotton.

Some of the state's farmers raise cattle. Arizona's grasslands provide good grazing for livestock. More than seven of every ten acres (3 of 4 ha) in Arizona is used for grazing cattle. Ranchers also raise hogs, chickens,

(opposite)
Farming is a major industry in Yuma, a city in the southwestern corner of Arizona.

54

and dairy cows. Only about three of every hundred Arizonans are ranchers.

## Mining

Arizona is rich in minerals, and mining has been an important industry since copper was first discovered in the 1850s. Almost two-thirds of all copper mined in the United States comes from Arizona. Copper is used in almost all electrical wires. It is also used to make brass and bronze and to make coins. Most of the copper mines in Arizona are in the southern part of the state.

## WHO'S WHO IN ARIZONA?

César Estrada Chávez (1927–1993) grew up in a family of migrant fieldworkers who moved from place to place raising crops. In 1962 he founded the National Farm Workers Association (later called the United Farm Workers of America), an organization that helped get better pay and improved working and living conditions for farm workers, including Hispanics. In 1994 he received the Presidential Medal of Freedom for his efforts. He was born in Yuma.

Gold and silver are also mined in Arizona, but they are not as important to the economy as copper. More than $80 million worth of gold and silver were mined in Arizona in 1996. Coal is mined on the Navajo Reservation, and oil has been found on Navajo land.

## Manufacturing

About nine of every hundred people in Arizona work in manufacturing. In 1998, the number of manufacturing jobs in Arizona increased dramatically, more than any other state in the nation. Most manufacturing plants are located in the Phoenix metropolitan area. Tucson is another growing manufacturing center.

America West, a major United States air carrier, has its headquarters in Phoenix.

Arizona's leading manufactured products are electrical equipment, computers, aerospace vehicles, and scientific instruments such as measuring devices. Transportation equipment, including helicopters and aircraft parts, are also made in Arizona. Companies such as Microage, Avnet, and Phelps Dodge make aluminum products, radios, televisions, electrical equipment, and computer parts. Chandler, south of Phoenix, has attracted companies such as Intel and Motorola. Chandler is quickly becoming a center of high-technology in the American west.

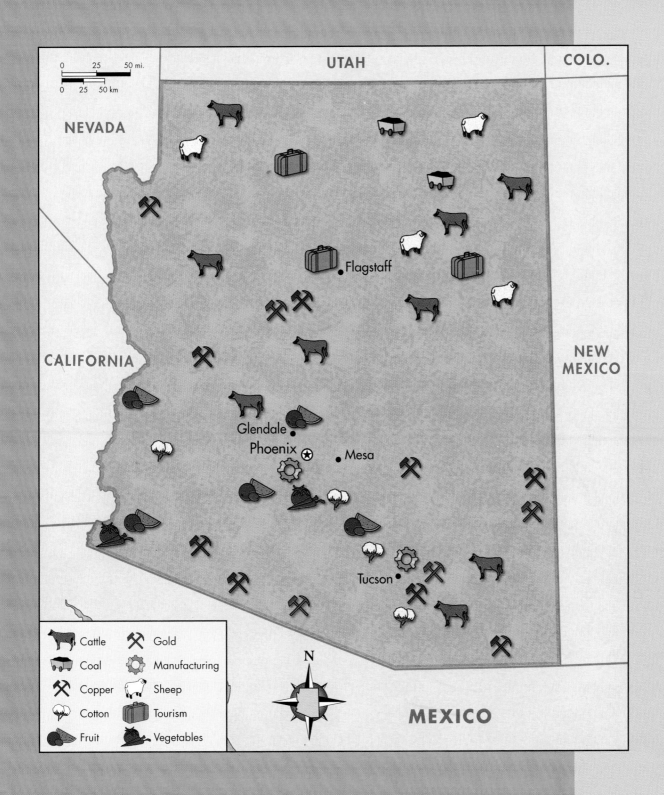

NEVER

UTAH

COLO.

NEVADA

CALIFORNIA

• Flagstaff

NEW
MEXICO

Glendale •
Phoenix ⊛    • Mesa

Tucson •

| | Cattle | | Gold |
|---|---|---|---|
| | Coal | | Manufacturing |
| | Copper | | Sheep |
| | Cotton | | Tourism |
| | Fruit | | Vegetables |

N

MEXICO

0   25   50 mi.
0   25   50 km

### Northern Arizona

The best place to start our tour of Arizona is the Grand Canyon, in northwestern Arizona. More than four million tourists visit the Grand Canyon each year. Most people go to the south rim of the canyon, but the view is spectacular from any point around it. You can hike to the bottom of the canyon or ride on mules. There is one hotel on the canyon floor called Phantom Ranch.

Twenty-one different layers of rock make up the canyon walls, which began forming more than a billion years ago. In 1919, the Grand Canyon was declared a national park to help preserve and protect its beauty for many years to come.

Backpackers descend a hiking trail at Grand Canyon National Park.

In north-central Arizona is the Petrified Forest National Park, where visitors can see fallen trees and tree trunks that have turned to stone. Some of the trees are up to six feet (2 m) in diameter. Because so many people took pieces of petrified wood out of the forest, the area was in need of protection and was declared a national monument in 1906. Today it is illegal to remove any petrified wood from the park. Within the park, visitors can stop at Agate House, a home built from petrified wood almost six hundred years ago. Two of the rooms have been partially restored to look as they did when it was first built.

Also located within the park is the Painted Desert. It covers about 7,500 square miles (19,425 sq km) and is best known for its brilliantly colored rock formations and fossils. At different times of day, the heat, light, and dust of the desert cause what seem to be changes in its color.

West of the Painted Desert is Flagstaff, the largest city in northern Arizona. It is located at the base of the San Francisco Peaks, which makes the city a popular ski resort in the winter. Visitors to Flagstaff can ice-skate, ski, and hunt. In summer, the city provides relief from the Arizona desert heat. Summer temperatures average

Downtown Flagstaff has a lot to offer, including a wealth of shops and restaurants.

(opposite)
The remains of pueblos at Wupatki National Monument stand several stories high.

twenty degrees cooler than in Phoenix.

The Lowell Observatory is located in Flagstaff. Percival Lowell and his sister built the observatory in 1894. For years, scientists have used its telescopes to observe the stars and the planets. Visitors to the Lowell Observatory can view interactive exhibits and take the Pluto Walk, a stroll past the planets in their order from the sun.

Native American history comes alive in Flagstaff. The Museum of Northern Arizona has exhibits about Native American peoples and a life-size reproduction of a kiva. At the Walnut Canyon National Monument, visitors can see cliff dwellings that are almost one thousand years old.

More cliff dwellings and pueblos are preserved at Wupatki National Monument. Archaeologists—people who study the artifacts of ancient cultures—have discovered more than 2,700 sites at the park where ancient Hopi and Navajo people once lived. They have also uncovered spear points more than ten thousand years old. Many areas in Wupatki are still considered sacred to the Native Americans.

Prickly pear cacti are found in the Arizona desert. Its pads and seeds can be used in lots of different recipes, from omelettes and pastry to salsa and jam. This sweet, chewy candy is a delicious way to enjoy a uniquely southwestern fruit. Remember to ask an adult for help!

## CACTUS CANDY

3 cups granulated sugar
1 cup water
2 tbsp. orange juice
1 tbsp. lemon juice
1 prickly pear cactus ear

1. Using a knife, remove the spines from the cactus, then remove the outside layer.
2. Cut the pulp across in slices one-inch thick.
3. Soak overnight in cold water.
4. Remove the cactus from water and cut it in one-inch cubes.
5. Cook the cubes in boiling water until they are tender; drain.
6. To make the syrup, heat sugar, water, lemon juice, and orange juice until the sugar is dissolved. Add cactus.
7. Cook slowly in syrup until nearly all the syrup is absorbed. Do not scorch! Remove cactus from syrup and drain.
8. Roll in granulated or powdered sugar. For colored cactus candy, vegetable food coloring may be added to the syrup.

## Central Arizona

Prescott, located in central Arizona, is the home of the nation's first rodeo. The rodeo started in 1888. Since then, riders from around the world have traveled to Prescott in hopes of winning prize money in events such as bull riding, bronco busting, calf tying, and roping.

Prescott is home to several museums. The Sharlot Hall Museum in Prescott features exhibits about human and natural history, dating from the 1800s to the present. The museum site includes several gardens and the governor's mansion, which is open to the public for tours. Also in Prescott is the Bead Museum, which displays a collection of beads, as well as jewelry and other items made from beads. An exhibit explains how beads were once used as a form of money. The Smoki Museum houses Native American artifacts such as jewelry and pottery. The building itself is designed to look like an Indian pueblo.

Lake Havasu City is located on Lake Havasu, at the border of western Arizona. A dam on the Colorado River created Lake Havasu. The lake is used for boating and fishing, and ferry service runs to the California side of the lake.

While the lake itself is beautiful, the London Bridge is the main tourist attraction in Lake Havasu City. The bridge connects the mainland to an island in the middle of the lake. The London Bridge was originally built over the Thames River in London, England. Years later,

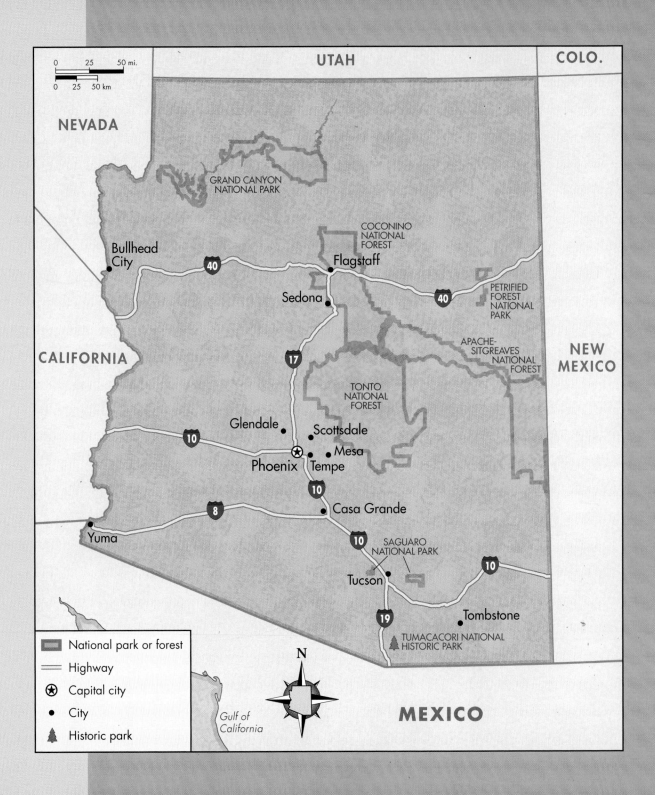

when the bridge was about to be demolished, Lake Havasu City bought it from the city of London. The bridge, originally built in 1831, is 49 feet (15 m) wide and 920 feet (281 m) long. It was shipped to Arizona in 1869 and rebuilt one brick at a time. You can get a taste of England at "English Village," an area of English-style shops and restaurants nestled under the bridge. Guests can ride on a double-decker bus and eat at an English pub, right in Arizona.

Thousands of visitors come to Lake Havasu City each year to see the London Bridge, which crosses the Colorado River.

## Southern Arizona

Arizona's second largest city, Tucson, has the largest Hispanic population in the state. This strong Mexican influence is evident in the style of the buildings. Spanish is spoken throughout the city.

The Arizona-Sonora Desert Museum in Tucson is a zoo, a natural history museum, and a botanical garden—all in one! It houses more than three hundred displays of desert animals, including mountain

A Mexican influence is evident in the architecture of historic Pima County Courthouse in Tucson.

lions, hawks, and Gila monsters, in their natural habitats. A limestone cave at the museum displays various gems and minerals found in Arizona.

The Kitt Peak National Observatory in Tucson has the world's largest collection of optical telescopes in the world. Daytime visitors can take a guided tour of the observatory. If you prefer to explore the night sky, visit shortly after sunset to participate in a nightly observing program. You'll get a close up view of the planets and stars through one of the telescopes.

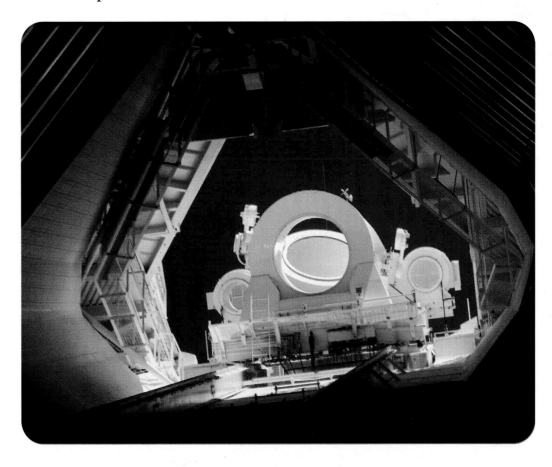

This solar telescope at Kitt Peak Observatory is the world's largest.

Many old western movies and television shows were filmed at Old Tucson Studios. The studio set is a replica of Tucson as it was in the 1860s. Guests to the studio can watch staged gunfights and take a ride in an old-fashioned stagecoach.

For more of the old west make a stop in Tombstone. This famous town in the southeastern corner of the state began as a mining town. The promise of quick riches brought many different kinds of people here, including outlaws, thieves, and gamblers. Tombstone is most famous for the legendary shoot-out at the OK Corral in 1881. The vic-

In the 1880s, Allen Street in Tombstone was the most notorious street in the west. Today it is home of the famous OK Corral and the Bird Cage Theatre.

tims of the shoot-out are buried in Boot Hill Graveyard. Visitors to the graveyard can buy souvenirs in the shape of tombstones.

There are many historic buildings in Tombstone. A short walk takes visitors past the *Tombstone Epitaph* building, home of the oldest newspaper in the country. The Bird Cage Theatre, built in 1881, was once a famous saloon and dance hall. The theater still holds its original furnishings. The Rose Tree Museum is the home of the world's largest rosebush—more than eight thousand square feet (744 sq m).

Arizona is a wonderful combination of striking scenery, diverse people, and many cultural and historical attractions. Far from being just a dry desert, Arizona is a fascinating place with a bright future.

# ARIZONA ALMANAC

**Statehood date and number:** February 14, 1912; 48th state

**State seal:** The state seal shows Arizona's major industries. A quartz mill and a miner represent the mining industry, and a sun behind a mountain peak represents the climate. A reservoir, cattle, and irrigated fields of cotton and citrus fruit trees represent agriculture. A shield with the state motto lies in the center of the seal. Adopted in 1912.

**State flag:** The bottom half of the state flag is dark blue. The top half has thirteen red and yellow rays for the original thirteen colonies of the United States, or for the thirteen counties that existed when the flag was designed. Red and yellow represent the time Spain ruled the area. In the center is a large copper star. Adopted in 1917.

**Geographic center:** Yavapai, 55 miles (89 km) east-southeast of Prescott

**Total area/rank:** 114,007 square miles (295,278 sq km)/6th

**Borders:** Utah, New Mexico, Mexico, California, and Nevada

**Latitude and longitude:** 31°N to 37°N and 109°W to 114°W

**Highest/lowest elevation:** 12,633 feet (3,851 m) at Humphreys Peak, Coconino County/70 feet (21 m) at the Colorado River, Yuma County

**Hottest/coldest temperature:** 128°F (53°C) in Lake Havasu City on June 29, 1994/–40°F (–40°C) at Hawley Lake on January 7, 1971

**Land area/rank:** 113,635 square miles (294,315 sq km)/6th

**Inland water area/rank:** 364 square miles (943 sq km)/41st

**Population/rank:** 5,130,632 (2000 census)/20th

**Population of major cities:**

**Phoenix:** 1,321,045

**Tucson:** 486,699

**Mesa:** 396,375

**Glendale:** 218,812

**Scottsdale:** 202,705

**Origin of state name:** From the Native American word *Arizonac*, meaning "little spring" or "young spring"

**State capital:** Phoenix

**Counties:** 15

**State government:** 30 senators, 60 representatives

**Major rivers/lakes:** Colorado River, Gila River, Salt River, San Pedro River, San Francisco River, Little Colorado River, Verde River, and Zuni River/Lake Mead, Theodore Roosevelt Lake, San Carlos Lake, Lake Havasu, Lake Powell, Lake Mohave, Apache Lake, Canyon Lake, and Saguaro Lake

**Farm products:** Cotton, hay, lettuce, citrus fruits, wheat, pecans, alfalfa, melons, dates, carrots, cauliflower, and beets

**Livestock:** Beef cattle

**Manufactured products:** Electrical equipment, machinery, metal products, printed materials, lumber, food products, and ceramic products

**Mining products:** Copper, sand, gravel, gold, petroleum, silver, gypsum, asbestos, pumice, uranium, mercury, and coal

**Amphibian:** Arizona tree frog

**Anthem:** "Arizona," written by Margaret Rowe Clifford and composed by Maurice Blumenthal (also called the "Arizona March Song")

**Bird:** Cactus wren

**Fish:** Arizona, or Apache, trout

**Flower:** Saguaro cactus blossom

**Fossil:** Arizona petrified wood

**Gem:** Turquoise

**Nickname:** Grand Canyon State, Copper State

**Mammal:** Ringtail

**Motto:** *Ditat deus* ("God enriches")

**Reptile:** Ridge-nosed rattlesnake

**Tree:** Palo Verde

**Wildlife:** White tail deer, mule deer, burro deer, northern elk, prong-horned antelope, big horn mountain sheep, buffalo, bear, mountain lion, jaguar, coyote, fox, badger, beaver, ocelot, otter, raccoon, muskrat, weasel, bobcat, jackrabbit, skunk, squirrel, chipmunk, deer mice, cottontail, shrew, rattlesnake, king snake, gopher snake, ground snake, western water snake, California blind snake, rosy boa, rock snake, keeled musk turtle, Arizona mud turtle, desert tortoise, Gila monster, chuckwalla, gecko, lizard, desert iguana, skink

# TIMELINE

## ARIZONA STATE HISTORY

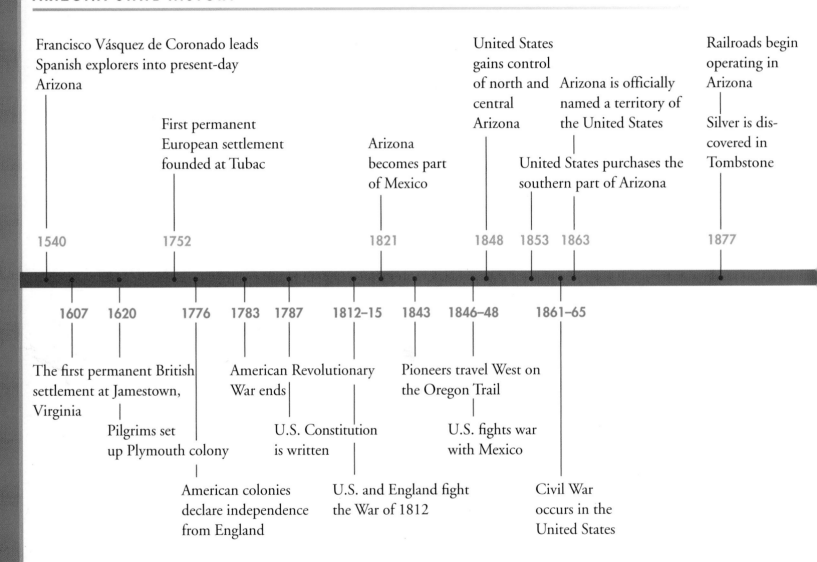

Francisco Vásquez de Coronado leads Spanish explorers into present-day Arizona

First permanent European settlement founded at Tubac

Arizona becomes part of Mexico

United States gains control of north and central Arizona

Arizona is officially named a territory of the United States

United States purchases the southern part of Arizona

Railroads begin operating in Arizona

Silver is discovered in Tombstone

**1540**    **1752**    **1821**    **1848**   **1853**   **1863**    **1877**

**1607**   **1620**    **1776**   **1783**   **1787**    **1812–15**   **1843**   **1846–48**    **1861–65**

The first permanent British settlement at Jamestown, Virginia

Pilgrims set up Plymouth colony

American colonies declare independence from England

American Revolutionary War ends

U.S. Constitution is written

U.S. and England fight the War of 1812

Pioneers travel West on the Oregon Trail

U.S. fights war with Mexico

Civil War occurs in the United States

## UNITED STATES HISTORY

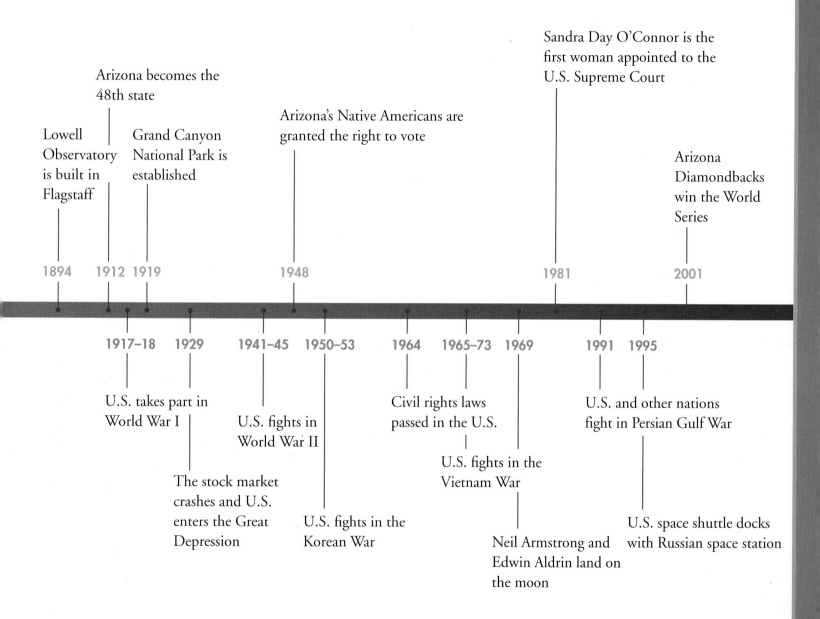

Sandra Day O'Connor is the
first woman appointed to the
U.S. Supreme Court

Arizona becomes the
48th state

Arizona's Native Americans are
granted the right to vote

Lowell
Observatory
is built in
Flagstaff

Grand Canyon
National Park is
established

Arizona
Diamondbacks
win the World
Series

**1894**　　**1912 1919**　　　　　　　**1948**　　　　　　　　　　**1981**　　　　　**2001**

**1917–18**　**1929**　　**1941–45**　**1950–53**　　**1964**　**1965–73**　**1969**　　**1991**　**1995**

U.S. takes part in
World War I

U.S. fights in
World War II

Civil rights laws
passed in the U.S.

U.S. and other nations
fight in Persian Gulf War

The stock market
crashes and U.S.
enters the Great
Depression

U.S. fights in the
Vietnam War

U.S. fights in the
Korean War

Neil Armstrong and
Edwin Aldrin land on
the moon

U.S. space shuttle docks
with Russian space station

# GALLERY OF FAMOUS ARIZONANS

### Cochise
(1810?–1874)
A Chiricahua Apache leader. After the United States government hanged four of his friends on a kidnapping charge that proved false, he led attacks against white settlers for many years. A county in southeast Arizona is named for him.

### Barry Goldwater
(1909–1998)
Served as a United States senator from Arizona for thirty years. In 1964, he unsuccessfully ran for president of the United States but reshaped American politics in the process. Born in Phoenix.

### Bil Keane
(1922– )
A cartoonist whose popular comic strip, *The Family Circus*, is printed in more than 1,500 newspapers. Lives in Phoenix.

### John McCain
(1936– )
Represents Arizona in the United States Senate. Previously served in the United States House of Representatives and campaigned for president in 1999. A leading defender of the rights of Native Americans. Lives in Phoenix.

### Rose Mofford
(1922– )
Arizona's first female governor in 1987. Previously served as Arizona's Secretary of State. Born in Globe.

### Charles Poston
(1825–1902)
Called the "Father of Arizona" for his role in convincing Congress to create the territory of Arizona. He was the first delegate to the United States Congress from Arizona. Lived in Tucson and Phoenix.

### Kerri Strug
(1977– )
Member of the 1992 and 1996 United States Olympic gymnastics team. She won a bronze medal in 1992 and a gold medal in 1996. Lives in Tucson.

### Frank Lloyd Wright
(1867–1959)
World-famous architect who designed buildings that fit within the nature surrounding them. Wright lived and worked part-time at Taliesin West in Scottsdale. The Frank Lloyd Wright Foundation's world headquarters are in Scottsdale.

# GLOSSARY

**adobe:** brick made of soil and straw and dried in the sun

**archaeologist:** a person who studies the artifacts of ancient cultures

**artifact:** an object made by human handiwork, especially primitive art

**butte:** an isolated, steep hill with a flat top

**cede:** to surrender

**constitution:** written document that defines the way in which a government is organized

**continental United States:** the name given to the forty-eight states that share borders with other states

**decipher:** to find out the meaning of

**diameter:** distance across a circle through its center

**discriminate:** to treat people differently because of the color of their skin or their religion

**drought:** a long period of dry weather

**ecosystem:** all the living and nonliving things in an area, such as water, soil, plants, and animals

**erosion:** the gradual wearing away of rock and soil by wind and water

**extinction:** the process of no longer existing or dying out

**fossil:** trace of a plant or animal that lived long ago

**Hispanic:** person of Spanish or Latin American heritage

**kachina:** one of many divine spirits that the Hopi Indians believed helped man communicate with the gods

**mesa:** a high, steep-sided rock plateau

**metropolitan:** relating to a major city

**migrant:** moving from place to place

**mission:** a place where missionaries work to teach religion in a territory or foreign country

**missionary:** a person sent by a religious group to teach religion or to help set up schools or hospitals

**Paleo-Indians:** "old" or "early" native people; the first known inhabitants of the Southwest were Paleo-Indians

**petrified wood:** wood that has gradually turned to stone

**petroglyph:** carving on a rock

**prejudice:** an opinion (usually unfavorable) that is formed without justification

**pueblo:** Spanish word for city or town

**reservation:** a piece of public land set aside by the government for the use of a group of people

**segregate:** keep separate

**slavery:** the practice of owning other people and forcing them to work against their will

**treaty:** formal agreement between countries

# FOR MORE INFORMATION

## Web sites

**Official Site of the Arizona Office of Tourism**
*http://www.arizonaguide.com*
Information about things to see and do in Arizona.

**Ghost Towns**
*http://www.carizona.com/ghosttowns.html*
A guide to Arizona's ghost towns.

**Governor Jane Hull's Kids Page**
*http://www.governor.state.az.us/kids/index.html*
A historical timeline of Arizona, and other state information including wildlife, state facts, and photographs.

**Arizona @ Your Service**
*http://azportal.clearlake.ibm.com/webapp/portal/*
A complete guide to Arizona's government, including cities and counties.

**Arizona Highways**
*http://www.arizhwys.com*
Includes photographs of Arizona wildlife.

## Books

Fraser, Mary Ann. *In Search of the Grand Canyon: Down the Colorado with John Wesley Powell.* New York, NY: Henry Holt & Co., 1995

Stein, R. Conrad. *The USS Arizona.* Danbury, CT: Children's Press, 1992.

Warren, Scott. *Cities in the Sand: The Ancient Civilizations of the Southwest.* San Francisco, CA: Chronicle Books, 1992.

## Addresses

**Governor of Arizona**
1700 West Washington
Phoenix, AZ 85007

**Arizona Office of Tourism**
2702 N. 3rd Street, Suite 4015
Phoenix, AZ 85004

# INDEX

## ABOUT THE AUTHOR

**Carole K. Standard** grew up in Bronxville, New York, and now lives in South Carolina. She is a graduate of the Georgia Institute of Technology and teaches high school mathematics. In addition to teaching, she coaches varsity swimming and is the school yearbook advisor. She lives with her two daughters, Karen and Allison, her husband Dan, and an English springer spaniel named Molly.